A
Balanced Life

A
Balanced Life

How to Achieve
Success in Every Area of Your Life

ANIS BLÉMUR

A BALANCED LIFE
HOW TO ACHIEVE SUCCESS IN EVERY AREA OF YOUR LIFE

MBA, Real Estate Broker & Instructor, Licensed Insurance Agent, Tax Practitioner, Public Accountant, CPA Candidate

iUniverse books may be ordered through booksellers or by contacting:

iUniverse
1663 Liberty Drive
Bloomington, IN 47403
www.iuniverse.com
844-349-9409

ISBN: 978-1-4620-6091-7 (sc)
ISBN: 978-1-4620-6092-4 (hc)
ISBN: 978-1-4620-6093-1 (e)

Library of Congress Control Number: 2011919548

Print information available on the last page.

iUniverse rev. date: 08/16/2023

Contents

Acknowledgement

Special Thanks to

Crystal Faith Valbrun
And
Jesusa Diaz,
For their drawings (not shown) which have been
digitalized by Nick Tellis, the digital drawer

Nick Tellis,
Digital drawer

Krystal Diaz,
Assistance in worksheet preparation and disposition;
disposition of illustration, as well

Gary Bourdeau
And
Max Desdusnes,
Photographers,

Max Desdusnes
Cover designer

Thanks to all who have inspired me, fully or partially

Love and Emotion

To my late mother, Nelta Georges Blemur, from whom I "borrowed" my beautiful last name. She is my "Shero." To my family and extended family, especially my sister Rolande Auguste, the Benjamin of the seven, whom I will never be able to pay back. She was the first one who commended me for my writing skills, even though I wrote her in French back in those days. To my sisters, Yrvine, Pierre-Marie, Chantale, and Anathalie, and to my brother Ary-lex, my true mentor, who never stopped studying.

This book is dedicated to all I have brought pain to, especially those I could not hear or understand when they were talking to me, from the heart.

To my children and grand children . . .

To my friends—all my friends . . .

Economy—Finance

To my employees, underpaid though they have been (Hope they don't sue.), from AB Fiancials.com, AB Consulting & Accounting Services, Inc., SuperTree Real Estate &

Investment Services, Inc., and ABI-Anis Blemur Institute, Inc.

From supervisors to the junior subordinates, you have made me who I am by keeping the vision going—by keeping ME running.

Education

To my great teachers and classmates from Maltide, Pre-K to "Les Frères de L'Instruction Chrétienne," College Notre-Dame, Miami Dade College, Florida International University, Barry University, and Nova Southeastern University

Spiritual

To my spiritual teacher, Tony Evans, who inspired me to teach over the radio waves and really taught me what Christianity is.

To my Ex-Pastors Rev. Marc St. Hubert and Rev. Joanem Floreal.

All of you helped me balance my life. I think of you all together—and when that happens, it brings nothing but joy and pride.

Half of this book's net proceeds will be donated to ABI-Anis Blémur Institute, Inc., a not-for-profit organization, for their continued efforts to improve and enhance the education system in the world, especially in Haiti.

Introduction

Welcome to *A Balanced Life!*

Allow me to introduce myself to you. My name is Anis Blémur. I was born in Haiti. I came to the United States at the age of nineteen after graduating from high school. After my graduation from Miami-Dade College in 1989 with an Associate of Arts degree in business administration, I enrolled in Florida International University and graduated in 1992 with a Bachelor of Science in finance. I went on to earn my Masters in Business Administration from Barry University in 2001 with a concentration in accounting.

Since graduating, I have worked my way up from bookkeeper and junior accountant at SER/IBM Institute to president and CEO of my own company, AB Consulting & Accounting Services, Inc.

I am also the owner and principal broker of SuperTree Real Estate & Investment, Inc., a Florida real estate corporation helping the international market acquire a piece of the Sunshine State, one dwelling at a time. In addition, I am the founder and chair of ABI-Anis Blémur Institute, Inc., a real estate school fully licensed by the state of Florida to offer courses online and in person.

It goes without saying that I am a jack of all trades. The best way to think of me is as a financial advisor and tax practitioner managing a real estate brokerage firm.

But that's just my educational and financial background.

I should also tell you that I am a born again Christian. I *try* to live by Christian principles.

I also *try* to give back to the community. I have served as chairperson of the Parent Leadership Council for the Miami-Dade County Public Schools for two years (2007-2009). I have also served as president of the youth ministries for two local churches.

I greet every day with a big smile! I have an enthusiasm for life that cannot be quenched—no matter what comes my way. I stay happy all the time. Life is too good to be grumpy, right?

Why do you need to know all of this? I believe that, through it all, I have achieved a balance life. Or there was a time I did.

No! I have achieved a balanced life. It gives me a sense of peace, fulfillment, and accomplishment.

And now I have a desire to give back to others and show them the way toward this lifestyle.

That's why I have written this book. It's time to take the lessons I've learned and make them available to everyone, everywhere—not just the people who I come in contact with every day.

When I came to the United States, I had nothing, but a high school diploma equivalent. But I built a wonderful life for myself. Not just through education. Not just through succeeding financially. Not just through knowing Jesus Christ. (By the way, this book is for everyone, not just Christians. You'll see why later.) Not just through being emotionally fulfilled. Through all of it . . . together, all at one time! I learned how to achieve and maintain a balanced life.

Do you know people who have money but are miserable? How about those with a great family and spiritual life who are broke? True happiness comes when you are able to maintain four areas I call the Essential Elements of Life: eternity, emotion, education and economy.

I realized there was a simple way for everybody to do this. I created a visual guide that people can use every day to move them closer to a balanced life.

People I showed it to loved it! They said it helped them positively change their way of life. It helped them make decisions in a new way and motivated them to do what needed to be done. They were happier and more fulfilled—in every aspect. *They were experiencing a balanced life!*

I am here to tell you that it doesn't matter where you were born. It doesn't matter what your family situation was growing up. It doesn't matter whether you were rich or poor.

Everyone needs a balanced life—and everyone can have a balanced life!

My wish for you is that you achieve your true potential. Not just in one area of your life, but in all areas. I want you to be financially, educationally, spiritually, and emotionally balanced.

Too many people have success in one or two areas, but they are miserable because of the imbalance in one of the others. There is a way to correct that—and I want to show you how.

Let's begin our journey together toward a balanced life!

Chapter 1

What is a Balanced Life?

I want to talk to you about your lives. Yes, I said lives—meaning more than one!

I say that because I believe there are many lives that people can live—many lives that people can choose to live. There are several ways to live. I call them lives because no one has only one life to live! That's what I believe.

Look at it this way: in politics, people can change from one political party to another. Good politicians explain to you that a democrat thinks and lives very differently from a republican. And an independent thinks and lives very differently from members of the other parties.

Some people work in factories for their entire lives. Others in the same line of work may decide not to continue in that industry and return to school to become educators. Now they are teachers—they are spending time thinking about how to teach, how to explain concepts and principles to others. In the factory, they were doing things that other people taught them through books or beliefs. This explains a life change situation that you are probably familiar with. If you do understand change, you know that the same people who make the same change could be living two different lifestyles: family time, socializing, savings, and spending money may increase significantly.

Note that there was a sacrifice to be made. While working, they had to go to school to further their education, or they had to quit work to pursue a higher learning horizon. This what's called opportunity costs, in economics: we have togive up something for another.

There are different types of lives—and that's at the core of the concept of a balanced life.

You Can Control Your Life

From 2008 to 2009, I had a weekly two-hour radio show called "The AB Show: How to Manage your Business, How to Manage Your Finance." Finance is only one of the elements of a balanced life, but I had to learn the hard way that it is not only about the money. To truly be happy and financially successful, you must have a balanced life.

You have a life now, but you have to identify what type of life you are living. Why? Because by identifying where you are in every part of your life, you can control it.

I mean it! You can control your own life. You have control over your life, but did you know that it is given to you?

When I say we all have many lives, I am talking about choices. You control your life by controlling your choices.

There is Power in Your Choices!

Life's Circus

You can choose so many different paths in life. There is a lot of power in our choices. Think about it: Our choices in life can lead us to a whole new wonderful way of living. Our choices can also destroy us. What really matters is that it's your choice!

You can even have a "zero" life. When you refuse or do not know how to make a decision about your future, you are at time zero (a pre-starting point). You do not want to be labeled, pigeonholed, or categorized. You want to keep all possibilities open at all times. By doing this, you really do not choose anything. You do not accomplish anything either. You stay with an ever-dwindling number of possibilities—until it's too late.

The life you have is up to you! You have power in your decisions. You need to pay attention instead of sailing along in life.

Not making a decision *is* a decision—a decision to do nothing, achieve nothing, and ultimately to die with nothing.

I don't want that for you. Instead, I want you to achieve the best life possible—and that comes from living a balanced life. It's about making choices—the *right* choices, at the *right time*. And I can help you do that!

What is a Balanced Life?

A balanced life is one in which all areas of your life are being controlled by you either during good or hard time; it's not when all things are going well. A balanced life is a life in which you have not only your finances balanced but also your spiritual life balanced, your emotional life balanced, and your educational life balanced.

And it's the direct result of making educated choices and staying focused. Having a balanced life is a daily choice!

It will take some painstaking time and work to achieve a balanced life. But it's worth it. You are worth it. I'm going to make it easy for you. I am going to introduce you to a tool that took me years of experience to create.

It's called A Balanced LifeWatch (or the AB Watch). Let it be your compass, pointing you to the way to a better, more balanced life.

Chapter 2

A Balanced Watch

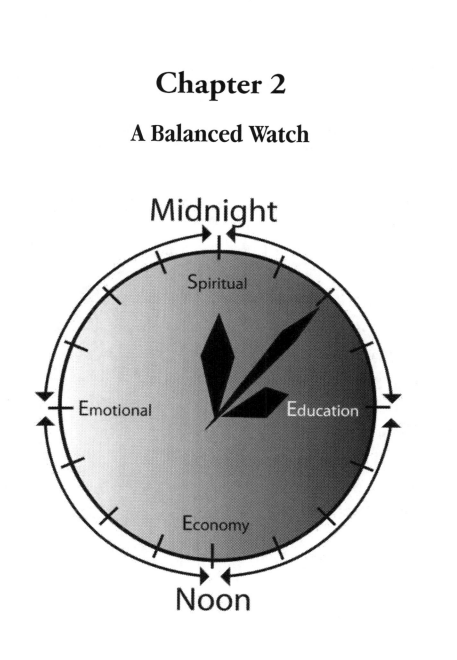

Every day is a new opportunity to change your life. You have the ability to change. Don't think so? Think again—change happens all the time!

People make physical changes. They lose or gain weight. They change their hairdos. Sometimes they even have surgery to change their physical appearance or to correct an internal abnormality.

People can also make mental changes—they can decide to be more or less loving, to be friendlier or more aloof, or to try to learn something new or start a new career.

People are changing spiritually—they find God, or they move away from Thee, or they finally find what they believe in.

You can change your life for the better too. You just need the right tools. Being able to visualize all of the aspects of your life at one time will help you.

The Four Quadrants of Life

A balanced life has four components:

1. Educational
2. Spiritual (Eternal)
3. Emotional
4. Financial (Economy)

The financial quadrant of life is how you manage and deal with your finances. However, that's not all there is to life. You may be financially strong—you may have more than enough money in the bank—but the rest of your life could still be a mess!

The spiritual quadrant is whoever or whatever you believe in that is larger than yourself. *Why are we here? What is the purpose of life?* These are questions you must answer to have the spiritual side of your life balanced.

The emotional quadrant refers to how you perceive your life and your relationships. Is a good marriage, family, and kids all you need for a balanced life? Not necessarily. Some people don't have a spouse or children, but they still are balanced emotionally through their rich friendships and social network. Some people who do have a spouse and kids think that it is not enough, that it's not perfect, and that there is someone else they want to be with. In this case, the person is not emotionally balanced.

The educational quadrant is different than you might think. Many people ask me questions such as: "What is education?" "How educated can you be?" "Am I really educated?" Basically, they want to know if educational balance means that you are an expert at many things. They want to know if they are supposed to have "a head full of stuff"—to know about everything that is going on.

Or should they streamline their knowledge—is education about what they already know?

Education is a combination of knowledge and how you carry out your daily life. You will find more on this in the education chapter!

ABW—A Balanced LifeWatch

The LifeWatch is a visual map of a balanced life. In the middle, there is a cross. At the top is the spiritual; on the bottom, finances. To the left is emotion, and to the right is education.

When you draw a circle around the four quadrants, it's in the shape of the face of a watch.

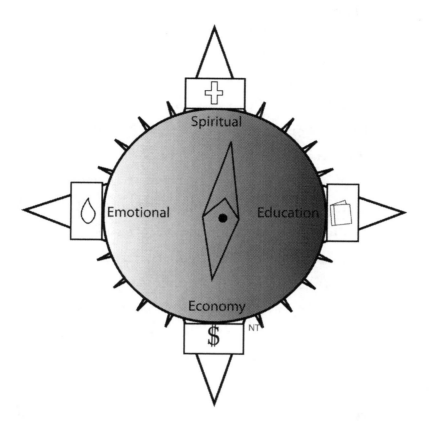

When you look at the LifeWatch, you can see that this is not a simple symbol. You are looking at a cross inside a circle. The circle represents your world. You are going to identify what you are putting inside the world and decide whether you are causing your life to be out of balance.

It's important for you to understand why I chose to depict this concept where life is balanced with an encircled cross.

The cross is at the roots of Christianity. Now, please understand that I'm not talking to only Christians. I have to explain myself so that you understand where I'm coming from. I've chosen to follow Jesus Christ. It's in accord with my belief. It doesn't have to be like that for you. Before I started following Christ—entirely by faith—I had to go "out" of Christianity to study and be skeptical about it and all other religions and look for what they offer at the end of the day. I realize that some religions offer reincarnation, others inertia. Only Christianity offers eternal afterlife life *with* a glorious body (which is the topic of my next novel); it is the only one within which one dies for all! No kamikazes! I don't have to die for anyone! Except for love of course, which is crazily normal! Therefore, I am going for this glorious body. I know what I can do with one. Don't you?

I choose this symbol in order for you to see what I envision. Again, I am not only talking to Christians—I am talking to anyone who wants a balanced life. In fact, I am looking at you right now—alive in the position of the cross—where you are holding education in your right hand, emotion on the left, letting the spirit coming from the top to inspire you, standing on the wealth that was long ago promised to you, as long as you continue to hang on to what you have and use them to educate and love others.

The cross can take you to a balanced life. It depends on how you want to follow this pathway. I do not see Jesus on the cross—I see you! Oh! So vulnerable, naked, and ready to take it! The big blow from life is at the center—full of knowledge and passion to embrace life and all it brings.

The cross is very important because it equally separates the quadrants, which represent the four basic elements of life. We are going to talk about each area of your life in more detail, but keep in mind the picture of the cross with a circle around it.

The circle represents your life and your world. It can be as big as you want it to be. If you think your world is small, the circle is small. If you think your world is big, the circle is big. We're going very far with this because this is your balanced life! We want to make it the best it can be, right?

Note that I am not replacing a normal life with a balanced life. However, I am identifying the different facets of life and combining them into only four manageable elements. Putting them together in a circle allows you to see your world in a more controllable way. In fact, the watch is how we live on a twenty-four-hour basis. In reality, these aspects aren't separate—they are always a part of life.

Let's look again more closely at this circle. The four quadrants represent four full aspects of your life.

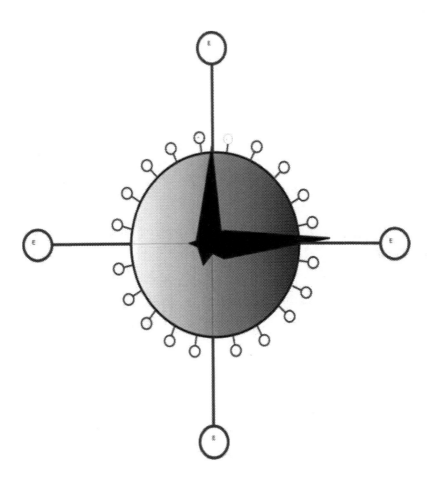

When you look at this graphic, it's like looking at the face of a watch. However, this is no normal watch—it's the watch of life. It has all the hours—not only twelve. You should be able to put everything that happens in your life somewhere in one of those four quadrants.

How We Live Our Lives

Different times of day are devoted to different quadrants of the ABWatch.

In the morning and the afternoon, it's education. It's when kids go to school. It's also finance time for adults—when most adults go to work.

At night comes the emotional part. When people are dating, that's when they see each other. It's also when we eat dinner—feeding ourselves and tending to the emotional sides of our beings. It's when we spend time with our families, reconnecting with our kids. Or we tend to ourselves emotionally after a tough day by tuning out in front of the television, working out, or reading a good book. It's all part of the emotional side.

When we go to sleep, the body gives up control to the spiritual. The latter takes over matter so that you may rest. Allow me to address a few spiritual leaders who fail to teach and encourage their followers about deep, long sleeps. Nowadays, they are more into a long night of prayers and cries. People need to understand that being asleep is being in the hand of a higher power who will decide whether you will come back to reality. After you fully understand this mystery, you will cease to wake up depressed, disappointed, or unprepared to embrace life. I am not saying that you will always come back ready. It depends on what is being done to you while you are sleeping. Depending on who you serve or worship during the daytime, you will encounter or experience different dreams or nightmares. No matter whom you serve or when you go to sleep, that period of time is not controlled by you.

We need to realize that life is divided into four parts—and the division is shown on the watch we wear.

The reality is that life is built upon those four elements. You cannot escape them—no matter what. The next step toward balancing your life is to know how to gain control over each of those elements.

What Happens When One Quadrant Takes Over?

Some people focus on one aspect of their lives and forget the rest—and that can cause serious trouble!

For example, some people are greedy for money. That's the extreme of the financial position. They say and do evil scams to get money—and end up most of the times hurting other people in the process. They may lie and cheat in business and end up in jail when someone blows the whistle. They may sink into a deep depression—or worse—because of stress and overworking caused by their attempts to get more and more money or by the devastating blow of losing money when something goes wrong.

Some people, on the other hand, have a love of sex. They are addicted—they have many mistresses or many girlfriends. They have an extreme interest in sex—and that's why they are always in trouble. But guess what? It seems that society doesn't understand what the problem is. Society often severely punishes those people instead of giving them emotional treatment to help them understand that an excessive interest in sex is an uncontrolled part of their lives and needs to be talked about. It's a problem that stems from not having a balanced life.

It's the same with pathological liars—they have an emotional imbalance. They let that quadrant take over the other three. It hurts them because no one believes or trusts what they say. They lose existing relationships and prevent new ones from happening because no one wants to be around them.

When people finally realize that there are other dimensions in life—and they see life for what it really is—they can learn to control their behaviors.

An extreme example of being out of balance is suicide. People who commit suicide do it because one element is dominating.

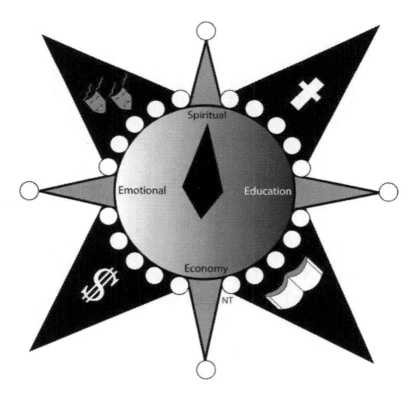

Remember the Branch Davidians? On April 19, 1993, fifty-four adults and twenty-one children killed themselves because they were following David Koresh and totally accepted his religious beliefs—they let the spiritual side take over their lives. They isolated themselves from the rest of the world—and had sex with each other and the pastor—because Koresh said that was the way it should be. They committed to the spiritual quadrant of their lives—and it caused them to make irrational decisions. Ultimately, it cost them their lives.

It's the same thing with finances. I have heard of brokers who had killed themselves when the stock market crashed in 1987. This is not a balanced life—they let the finance section take over. For them, it was all about money, money, money. The tragic part is that the stock market eventually regained its losses and closed up at the end of the year. If they had kept their emotions balanced—just for a few months—they would have been okay.

You don't have to die for money; you don't have to die for anything! When you have a balanced life, you can weather all of life's storms better. And you will come out on top!

The LifeWatch is Your Tool

You can use the imagery of the LifeWatch to guide you to success. When you look at it, you can start assessing your life based on each element. Do not hesitate to write down what is going in your life according to each quadrant. I have attached a checklist at the end of each section as a guide that will allow you identify your strengths and weaknesses while walking toward balancing your life. It helps you to get a visual check on what is happening—and it will help you to keep the balance.

When the stock market crashes again, there will be a *financial* imbalance. However, you shall think of your family to secure or bring them comfort, *emotionally*. You will have to remind them or inform them that those crises are not uncommon—they had happened, but they are temporary—soundly *educating* them about the past, bringing them hope. You will be surprised to see a few, finding recourse through *prayer and worship* since they will find themselves powerless and unable to reverse the financial debacles. Note how you can use one element to strengthen the others. The secret is to use the elements that you control the most to empower the others; you can work on rebuilding any sector that is not going so well. You don't want to give up and commit suicide because you still have three areas of your life to live for!

Did I ask you to go see a priest, a sex counselor, a dean, or a financial advisor? No! I ask you to "reach within your inner self" to what you know, your controlled feelings, and or your beliefs to come to the *rescue* of the weak elements.

You must constantly look at your watch to see what time it is in your life and decide swiftly or slowly, what to do.

Looking at the ABWatch regularly will help you achieve a balanced life. Just by watching it, you can see what you need to work on (what time it is not). When you are faced with a decision, you can gaze at it and ask yourself, "What would happen to each area of my life if I did this?" And then you will have your answer.

What Success Really Is

What does success really mean? It's not your bank account! It's a deep and abiding sense of peace. That peace comes from living or walking toward a balanced life.

A balanced life is not about being rich. It is not about being a preacher. It is not about being a genius. It's not about being an ideal husband or a wealthy investor. It's about satisfaction, peace, and a life well lived!

Whether you are rich or poor, whether you are a scholar or you don't know how to read or write, whether you are single or married—once you have a balanced life, you have peace!

When you have a balanced life, you walk with a sense of knowledge and hold your head high to meet people and greet them with confidence. Having this attitude, you are telling them that there is hope for them, too.

The message is the importance of a balanced life. You are giving other people hope that life can be better than what they think. There is a better way to life!

Are you ready to find out how to get a balanced life? Great! The time is now. Let's start with education.

Chapter 3

Education

North Dade College Campus

BLDGA

Education is the key to a balanced life. However, before you run off and enroll in school again, let's make sure my definition of education is the same as yours!

What Education Is—and Isn't

Education is what you have learned from the school bench *and* from the bus bench in preparation for embracing life, itself. It is not all about schools and degrees, but they can be a part of it. It's more about how you prepare for and operate in life.

Do you show up to a job interview without knowing anything about the company? If you educate yourself first, you have a better chance of getting the job.

Do you become a hairdresser without getting the training and the licensing? Sooner or later, that will hurt you. Someone will find out—and you won't be able to do that anymore.

Do you try to create a computer program without knowing the programming language? It's impossible!

But to be educationally balanced, you don't have to know all things!

You Don't Have to Know Everything

Education doesn't mean that you must know every single thing that is going on. There's no way you are going to know everything about every type of art, every field of science, and every profession. You have to specialize in something!

If you do not know what to specialize in, you will have to look into your past to see what you've studied in various subjects. Pick one that interests you and that you did well in—you may be surprised how many times they are the same one.

It's What You Do With What You Know

What do I mean by a balanced education? It doesn't matter whether you went to school, have a degree, have a graduate degree, have a PhD, or a certain certification. What matters is how you control the degree you have earned. How do you control what you know, and how do you control what other people know? That's what makes you an educationally balanced person.

Educational balance doesn't come from what you know or from your degrees. It comes from how well you control your degree, knowledge, or education—and how well you use it to balance your life.

It is impossible to know every single thing. If you try to learn everything, you will go mad. You don't need to do that. What you need to know is this: Based on what you know, how well are you controlling it?

Some people don't have the education, but they become mentors. They don't have a university degree to back up their knowledge or their education. But guess what? They control what they have.

Musicians are another example. Many of them are high school graduates or even dropouts, but they have control over their knowledge. What they know they put into music, lyrics, and rhythm. Guess what? People are listening to them—and buying their CDs!

At the end of the day, you need to know how you are going to control your education in order for it to become a tool for success.

Education is Picking and Choosing

Again, education is not knowing everything. On the contrary, it's picking and choosing.

It's picking and choosing what you believe in and what you like—and then developing it. It's making sure that whatever you believe in—whatever you choose—that you understand it, embrace it, and follow up on it.

For example, don't tell me that you are a Realtor and you can't visualize ten miles—or even ten yards! Don't tell me that you don't know the metric system? You are going to be embarrassed when you are invited to a meeting with civil engineers—and you don't even know about the measurements of the properties you are representing!

If you are in real estate, you are selling houses and properties. That means you should make it your priority to know everything about real estate in general and those properties in particular. Now, you are not a computer programmer, so you don't have to worry about learning how to write software. What you need to do is learn everything about real estate.

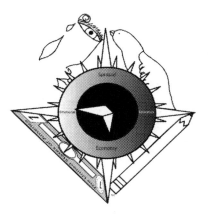

As a Realtor, you should be able to visualize the size of a room. When they say that a room is 10 x 10 or 10 x 12, you should be able to visualize a room that size. When a client calls and rattles off a list of what he wants, you need to recognize and understand the details. If he says he wants a family room that is 20 x 12 and you show him a property with a family room that is much smaller, that's not being a good Realtor. You didn't know your stuff! You need to go and learn it to be successful.

That's what I'm talking about with education. If you chose a field, educate yourself in it. If you continue growing in it, you will continue to make a good living doing it. That's the goal of education.

It's the same for me. I chose to teach accounting and finance, so I have to be on the ball all the time. I have to go to seminars. I have to go to conferences. I have to read all of the new books. I have to do what it takes to be up to date in accounting and finance to provide the latest and most accurate news to those I am servicing, to inform them about current situations, and to offer advice on the subject that I am teaching.

Education Doesn't Come by Faith

It is important to understand the difference between the spiritual and the educational sides of life.

When it comes to education, nothing comes by faith. Everything is technical. You have to know the facts, the subject, and what to say. You have to be accurate. You have to be on the ball!

For instance, if you quote somebody, the quote must be accurate. A lot of people quote other people and don't really know why. You'll see that I rarely quote anyone. Why? Because before I even think about quoting someone, I need to know the concept, exactly what that person said, why he said it, at what time, and at what location. It is important for me to be precise about what I'm saying. You should do the same!

Why You Should be Educationally Balanced

I am always very careful with the words I choose. I have to go back and think, "Is this really what I mean? Have I used this word before? Is it in the dictionary?" You don't have to go that far! But my point is that education is crucial for balancing your life.

So I was very careful in choosing the name for *A Balanced Life*. I wanted balance to be included because it's very important to me.

For instance, I'm talking about education now. If I am well educated, you know what can happen for me. Once I know all I am supposed to know in a particular field, success will come.

For example, if I am an engineer, I can build wonderful, well-made houses. Even if the money hasn't come yet—it will eventually. It will come because I know what I'm doing. I know my stuff! I love it. I enjoy it.

When somebody comes to look at the house, I know the measurements by heart. I don't need a pen to work the equation or a computer to run the figures—I know my houses and my designs inside and out. When customers ask me questions, I can answer them. I'm good at what I do and very well educated—they can see it. Guess what? I start to boost my whole life! I start to sell those houses.

If I don't have balance yet, I am just building up that one side of life. Building up one side can also support the other sides; in this case, the educational side is helping to boost the financial side. Emotionally, I am being helped too. I am not stressing out because I know I am ready for any opportunity!

What Happens When the Educational Side Gets Out of Balance?

Let's go back to the engineering example. Have you ever seen a great engineer who dresses like a crazy person? Who doesn't have a family? Who doesn't have a life outside of work? All he has is that particular side of life; he doesn't care about people. All he does is go to work and *maybe* take his boat out to go fishing. For him, nothing else matters. Sometimes he feels so driven to work that he doesn't even have friends. Because people cannot speak his language, he doesn't let them into his life. He is gradually isolating himself—and he doesn't even see it.

So that is not being in balance. Yes, the education is there—but nothing else is. That is not a balanced life.

For me, it would be easy to slip into being unbalanced educationally. I am educated—I have a bachelor's degree and an MBA. I know several languages. I can pick the perfect word to express what I mean. I know exactly what to say. When I am invited to give a speech, the word gets out—and the place is packed. People love it and say, "Oh, *he's* coming!"

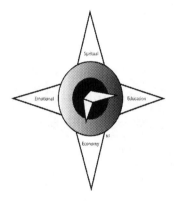

But guess what? Emotionally, I can still be unbalanced. Getting a big ego because one side of your life is going well will throw your life off balance in a hurry! It is not balanced if after a speech, you ask me about another subject, and I am rude to you! It is not balanced if other people can't even talk to me because I have a sticker that I put on my back that reads "Education Only!"

I teach about having an education, but if I only have that, I am not there yet! There is so much more to life.

Education is the Foundation of a Balanced Life

Education is one of the greatest vehicles for producing a balanced life. It supports all the other areas of life.

By educating yourself, you can get ahead financially. It allows you to follow your chosen profession and experience success in it.

Some people may be weak when it comes to spiritual beliefs, but education can help them find what they don't know. By learning what they believe and how to practice it, they are building themselves up spiritually.

Some people are emotionally weak—not because they are born that way but because they lack an education. Many times when you get education, you can control emotion. You can learn a better way to react to stress and troubles in your life.

Education is important because it allows you to balance your life financially, emotionally, and spiritually.

Chapter 4

Emotion

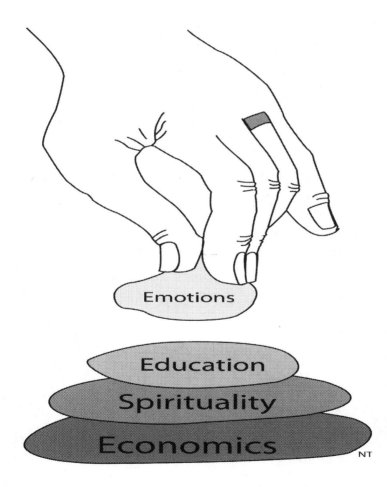

Emotion is something that has given humans problems ever since we began to walk the earth.

Unfortunately, because we don't see emotions as important—if we have never have seen it as something we need to balance—they can take control over everything else in our lives.

An emotional person is somebody who lets emotion, love, or passion control the rest of his or her life.

In reality, you are going to have emotions, but you also have reason. Reason is there to help you balance your emotions. Most people who are emotionally unbalanced are letting their emotions overpower their reason.

It's easier to understand by looking at the most extreme examples.

An example is a man who lets everything go because he found someone he loves. He lives for this love; she is all he talks or thinks about. He starts neglecting his work. He stops hanging out with his friends. He leaves everything behind because he has found this person. He is not balanced; he is an emotional person.

Another example is someone who has been married fifteen times. It may be that this person needs to realize that marriage is not for him. Or maybe he is not looking for somebody who wants stability, or maybe the other people are not stable. In fact, the person with fifteen marriages is probably not stable!

Out of Control Emotions Can Lead to the Zero Life

You have to be able to identify your emotions—and to recognize them for what they are. You do not have direct control over your emotions, but you need to control how you react to them. Otherwise, you will end up with a life that is out of control—a life where your options are limited!

That's one of the reasons why I mentioned earlier that there are many ways to live. Because there are many ways to live, there is another thing you have to consider. We've talked about this before. There is one option that we call zero life—it's no life. Those are the people who are not living.

Why should there be a life called zero? You mean nothing when you say zero. Some people don't have a life. The reason they don't have a life is that they are making other people miserable. Since they are miserable, they don't care about other people's lives—or their options. They want to stay stuck at zero—as miserable as it is. When you see this, there is a problem!

How do you know when you are there? You are not happy. People living with you are not happy—what you do emotionally affects them in a negative way. You may think you are happy, but you are not. You may think others are making you happy, but they are not. The problem can be hard to recognize.

You have to stop! Identify where you are emotionally. What are you feeling? What are your emotions doing to the other areas of your life? Listen to the other people in your life and ask them if  they think something is wrong. Sometimes other people can see things we can't, particularly those who are closest to us.

It is important to understand that emotion plays a big part in your life and in the lives of those around you. Because decisions based on emotion can make a big mess out of your life, you have to control emotion as much as you can!

How to Control Your Emotions

The only way you can control any one element of life emotions is to put the other three quadrants ahead of it.

The LifeWatch is a tool that will allow you to analyze the decisions you are making. It even lets you see into the future. It lets you see how another part of your life is going to be affected by your decisions. You can see how other parts of your life may go out of balance if you take a certain path—and you might just find that it's not worth it in the end. This is where reason comes in!

Look at your LifeWatch and ask, "If I make this decision, how is it going to change my life?" Really think about the ramifications to yourself and others. Whatever you are going to do, you have to make sure you control your emotion—or all other three aspects will be controlled by your emotion.

Let's look at an example—this time emotions will take a back seat (emotions have to be controlled and balanced—not killed!). It's a form of being out of balance emotionally when you ignore them altogether. Again, it's about balance.

Let's say you decide not to have kids. *I'm a teacher. I deal with kids all the time. I'd rather not have kids of my own. I will love other people's kids. My own kids would jeopardize my job performance.*

This situation could be very real, but I have to ask you about the other three aspects of life.

Will those kids you teach play a role in your life for the rest of your life? After you are done teaching those kids who are not yours, is it going to be okay with you to not have children of your own? Remember you are working as a teacher to survive, make money, and have a retirement. Is that going to be enough? Is it going to be okay that you didn't have kids? Maybe. Again that depends on you.

I want you to look at it with the right perspective—through the LifeWatch. Ask yourself if you will be emotionally, spiritually, educationally, and financially balanced with every decision you make. Only then will you make the right decision for yourself.

A similar example is a man who leaves his wife and kids for another woman. He probably feels happy at the moment he leaves. Emotionally, he felt he had to make a decision. Emotionally, he felt he had to doing something different. Emotionally, he wants to go and explore. But guess what? The rest of his life will be affected. Financially, he will suffer loss. Spiritually, he has not held to a higher power. Educationally, he has probably been distracted and thrown off course by this new woman.

It boils down to this: When you make one decision, you can't *not* consider the rest of your life!

It's not just "Oh I'm not going to get married because I'm studying," or "I don't believe in marriage," or even "I'm not going to get married right now because I don't have any money." If it will cost you the love of your life because you made a financial decision not to marry, then you are not going to be in emotional balance. One day, you might look back and regret that decision!

Make sure to consider all four elements of life in the decisions you make.

Chapter 5

The Spirit

Everyone needs to believe in something larger than himself.

You may say you don't believe in anything outside of yourself. Instead, you believe only what you can see, touch, taste, or feel. That is your choice. After all, it's your life! Just know that even the decision not to believe in anything is believing in something!

It's like those people who live a zero life because they refuse to make choices. They end up living a life one way or another—by not choosing, it is chosen for them. A nothing life *is* their choice!

There is a Spiritual Side to Every Life

If you have everything you want but don't believe in anything—if you are ambivalent about the spiritual aspect of life or ignore it altogether—then you will always feel that something is missing. And ultimately, you won't have a balanced life.

Whether you know it or not, you spend time every night with your spiritual side. In fact, while you are sleeping, the spiritual side is controlling your body. That's why your dreams sometimes have messages for you. It's your spirit sending you that message. Have you ever had a dream that told the future? I know many people who have. It is just one example of how dreams are much more than a byproduct of your daily life. Dreams are coming from something outside of your daily self—something that is trying to communicate with you.

When someone dies, what is missing from the body? It is the spirit. The organs can still be there—but they don't work without the spirit. Everyone has a spirit, but not everyone is aware of it or in touch with it.

If you start to pay attention to the spiritual—and find what you believe in—you will feel a sense of purpose and peace.

What I Believe

I have said before that this book is not just for Christians. It's for everyone. Anyone and everyone can live a balanced life.

Let me tell you, though, what Christianity has done for me and why I believe in it.

You've heard about religions where many people are supposed to die in order for one person to reach the ultimate—*a lot* of people are supposed to die for that one person to get there. I'm not going into details and I'm not naming names, because I am only explaining what I believe and I don't want to offend anyone. At any rate, in some other religions, for one person to reach the ultimate point, he has to kill many people. I don't know about you, but I don't believe in that.

With my beliefs, however, only one person died for everyone else to reach the ultimate. That's what I like. It's not because I'm a weak person—maybe I am, who knows? But I don't believe in death, and I don't believe anybody else should die for me. I know death is a passage—trust me on that. Even if Jesus didn't tell me that—even if the Bible didn't tell me that—I would know that.

Again, what struck me the most about Christianity was the way you get to salvation—through one person, and the price has already been paid.

Let's look at the other side of it. If I hadn't found Christianity, I would have declared myself a god. Now because there is Christ and I know there is God, I cannot be a god. I realize it is better for me to humble myself and go through Christ to get to God.

And that's what I'm saying—I would have been a god if God didn't exist. I think that the world is built perfectly—so perfectly that I'm putting together this book. At the end, you'll see the perfection you will reach—that we will reach together—and the concept of a balanced life.

I tell you all of this so that you can make your own decisions. Everyone has to choose for himself. Find what you believe in.

We can agree that we will all die one day. What is our purpose here? Is it all for nothing? Are we just an accident? What happens after we die? Are we simply gone—or do we live on in another form? These are questions people carry around with them—unconsciously or consciously—that their spirit longs to have answered. Find your path and follow it.

What Being in Balance Spiritually Can Do for You

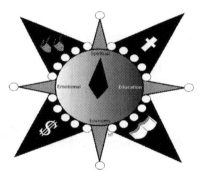

Try this for motivation to get your spiritual life in balance:

Studies show people who engage in spiritual activity live longer, are happier and healthier, and even make more money!

The August 1999 *Journal of Gerontology: Medical Sciences* published the results of one of the many, many studies that have been conducted on religious people. They found that once a week were less likely to die in any given period than those who went less frequently. Incredibly, the people in the study were 64 to 101 years old! *Incredible!*

It's also been shown that people who participate in religious activity have less depression and less anxiety. They also have lower blood pressure and fewer strokes. They typically rate themselves as "feeling healthier" than those who do not participate in religious activity.

In 2005, an economist found that households whose members attended religious services at double the rate of the members of other households had 9.1 percent more income. Welfare rates also decreased by 16 percent in the more active group. And to show you that being in balance contributes to your emotional life, check this out: The chances of being married increased by 4 percent and the chances of being divorced decreased by 4 percent among the more active religious group.

You see, every aspect of life builds on the other! Your spiritual side will help boost all other areas of your life.

What Being Out of Balance Spiritually Does to You

When you are out of balance spiritually, you will have a disastrous outcome. As I mentioned before, there were the Branch Davidians. But unfortunately there are other examples.

Take Jonestown, for instance. The members of the Peoples Temple followed Jim Jones from San Francisco to the jungles of Guyana, South America. They lived in isolation without any contact with the outside world. On

November 18, 1978, when Jones felt threatened that his community was being infiltrated, he had the visitors killed (including a Congressman). Then he killed himself with a gunshot—*after* having gotten 908 other people to commit suicide by drinking tainted Kool-Aid. *Even children.* This is horrible!

Thankfully, examples like these are few and far between. In your life, it is most likely not quite that extreme!

It may be someone who never leaves the church—or goes to every meeting, service, fundraiser, bake sale, committee meeting, and special event—and neglects kids and family. This can lead to divorce and lack of a relationship with children.

It may be someone who quits a job so that the "Lord can take care of me." The Lord will take care of you, but He does not want your hands to be idle! If you can work and you have a job, you should work. You may find yourself in poverty otherwise.

It can also be someone who studies only the Bible, ignoring what he needs to learn for his profession. You need *both* to have a balanced life! You will not perform well in your career if you don't stay informed and up to date—and you may even lose your job or your business because of it.

Life wasn't meant to be lived on a solely spiritual level. That's what heaven—and the afterlife—is for. We are here and now, and we also need to deal with the other aspects of life.

In fact, it's time to deal with what is on a lot of people's minds these days. It's time to deal with our finances.

Chapter 6

Finances

I saved finances for last for two simple reasons.

First, if you concentrate on improving your finances before getting other things in order, you might be tempted to ignore all the other areas of life. Although you may get wealthy under this scenario, you won't feel happy or fulfilled.

Think about people who've spent their whole lives chasing money. Movie stars, rock stars, and TV stars who've gotten ahead in their career—then at forty or fifty, they look back and are upset because they don't have a loving spouse or a family. They don't even have real friendships—it's all based on their fame and their money. They look up and realize there is more to life. How many stars wind up ruining their lives in spite of fame and fortune?

In New York and other cities, an overwhelming number of successful, single, and over forty women want to settle down. You can still take action if you are out of balance at any stage because life doesn't end at forty! However, they have let their finances get them out of balance by ignoring the other areas of their lives. They aren't living balanced lives.

I'm sure you can agree that some people have completely ignored the financial area of their lives. They are in debt, going through bankruptcy, or have zero in their bank account. This is the other extreme of being financially out of balance.

Of course, you don't have to be a millionaire to be financially balanced. Many people who don't have much materially are rich in other ways. They have enough resources to allow them to live the life they want; to them, they are balanced financially—and they live a balanced life.

Being too focused on finances—or not focused enough—can cause problems in life.

The second reason I delayed talking about finances until the end is because of what happens when you give money to people who aren't financially balanced. If they aren't balanced, the money will either make them miserable or will seem to take wings and fly away.

What Happens When You Give Money to People Who Aren't Financially Balanced?

It's not how much money you make; it's what you do with the money. If you know someone who is unbalanced, you can't fix their problem by giving them money.

In fact, they might lose it all! They need to be financially balanced—and being balanced in other areas (most notably, their emotions) doesn't hurt either.

Evelyn Adams won the New Jersey lottery—twice! She had $5.4 million—and now it's all gone. Her problem?

Gambling—and not being able to say no to constant requests by others for money.

Gambling is an addiction that needs to be treated. It is a form of being out of balance financially. Learning to say no—and keeping your money—is a financial balancing basic!

Evelyn is by no means alone. William Post won the Pennsylvania lottery and was awarded a huge sum—$16.2 million. He now lives on Social Security! At one point, he was in debt for $1 million—until he declared bankruptcy.

Suzanne Mullins won $4.2 million in the Virginia lottery. How did she lose her fortune? Instead of taking an annual payout and being satisfied with it, she borrowed money (using her win as collateral). When the law changed so that she could take a lump sum, she stopped paying the loan. That, as well as some family medical expenses, hurt her.

Ken Proxmire won the Michigan lottery, taking home $1 million. It's not $4 or $16 million, but you'll take it, right? Anyway, Ken started a business in another state—and filed for bankruptcy five years later!

I could go on and on. The point is that—unless you achieve financial balance—all money that comes your way will be lost.

"A fool and his money are soon parted," goes the old saying. So don't be a fool! Let's get you financially balanced!

We've been through getting educationally, emotionally, and spiritually balanced. Now, with everything else in your life under control, it's time to tackle your finances. Get ready! Here's your step- by- step action plan.

Your Step- by- Step Action Plan

Budget yourself.

You can use paper and pencil or pen or start a spreadsheet. Write down—or enter—your income. Make sure to put in your net income (what you get paid after taxes). It's the amount that you take home every week if you are employed. If you are getting income from another source, determine how much of that you have left after taxes. Put in the monthly amount, which is the sum of two paychecks if you are paid twice a month. If you are paid every two weeks, still put in the amount of two paychecks because that's all you get on most months. On the two months where you happen to get three paychecks, use the third check for your debt and your savings account (more on that later).

Write down everything you spend in an entire month. Keep all of your receipts or use one credit or debit card for everything so that, when you get the statement, you'll be able to determine how much you spent on each category. Enter it all into your spreadsheet or write it all down. Put like items together, for example, all food expenses and all gas expenses.

Subtract your expenses from your monthly take-home income. If the number is positive, great! You have something to work with. If it's negative, watch out! You are spending more than you make. Don't panic, we can fix it.

Cut expenses to get some cash to work with.

Are you spending more than you make?

If you are spending too much, figure out where to cut back. Establish a limit on each type of expense. For example, let's say you now spending $500 on food, and you are going to cut that down to $350. To do that, you may need to stop eating out as much. Eating lunch out every day instead of bringing it to work can get expensive! You may also need to buy generic brands at the grocery store or buy less expensive food in general. Sometimes switching to a discount store can shave some money off your grocery bill.

Or let's say you can get your gas expenditure down to $100 a month. To do this, you might have to walk instead of driving to some places. Or maybe you will have to stay home more in order to save on gas.

Make saving money a game. You can play it by rewarding yourself with a treat when you reach a certain goal. Or you can compete with your spouse or your children. See who can save the most money at

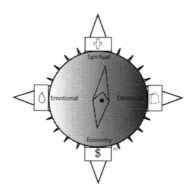

the end of the month. Have them look for opportunities to save money and give them a small reward for doing so. It's more fun if everyone is involved!

Cut down on debt while building your savings.

You can't do one or the other—you have to do both. Why? Because your sources of income could dry up overnight and you might need that cash. Believe it or not—many people don't see a layoff coming. Instead of doing one or the other first, do both at the same time. Divide the cash you've saved in Step 2 in half. Put one half toward repaying your debt and the other half into savings that you can access if you have an emergency.

Each month, compare your budget with what you actually spent. Make corrections as you need to. As you see your savings start to add up, you'll have motivation to continue.

When your debt is paid off, that does not mean you have more money to spend. Instead, put the extra toward your savings account. Once you have enough in your savings account to live on for a year without any additional income, it's time to start investing in vehicles (stocks and bonds) that can beat the interest you are earning on your savings account.

Give!

And don't forget to give! People who give more get more. Does this surprise you? It shouldn't. I've seen it in action in my clients' lives—and other financial advisors confirm that they've seen it over and over in their clients' lives as well. If you want to be rich, give money away. It's a natural law that will always work—people who give more get more!

This is a balanced approach to finances! If you follow this simple plan, you will bring your finances into balance—and you will have completed the final stage of our passage toward a balanced life. Congratulations!

Chapter 7

Tips **for a** Balanced Life ·

How to attain the American dream

Economics

Spirituality

Education

Emotions

Equality

The American Dream

My friend, it's been a pleasure walking with you on this journey. I hope you have learned and grown through this teaching.

I want you to know the most important thing about having a balanced life. If I had to choose one thing for you to learn from this book, it would be this: *Don't have a one-quadrant existence. If you are successful in one area—but neglect the others—you will suffer.*

Just having the knowledge of how to get money isn't going to make you rich. You have to be in balance in all areas of your life to keep, maintain, and grow wealth.

Just getting in touch with your spiritual side and finding what you believe won't make your life complete—unless you pay attention to other sides of life.

Having an education is not enough either. You can have the best education in the world, but you have to go out to get the finances and balance the emotional and spiritual side of life as well.

What is a Balanced Life Really About?

A balanced life is not about getting more in life. It's about taking what you have and making the most of it. It's about maintaining the balance that will make you happier and give you peace.

A balanced life is not the ultimate goal—it's actually a beginning! It gives you the proper view of life—the perspective you must have before proceeding any further. It's a guide—a map—to keep you on track.

With this guide, you are now prepared for life. But the next step is to take action!

A Balanced Life Prepares You

A balanced life prepares you to start living well. It prepares you for what lies in the future—everything that is beyond today.

During the olden times in African countries, when a young lady was preparing to marry a young man, certain things had to be completed first. The man was supposed to have a piece of land where he could work and make money. He had to be able to support his future wife and family before he could get married. On the other hand, the wife was supposed to know all about the man—without touching or talking to him. So the family "taught" the young bride about the groom's temperament—his likes and dislikes—so that the adjustment period was less stressful for him. He could continue to provide for his family with minimal pain!

It's the same for you. Having a balanced life gets you prepared to go to the next level—with minimal pain.

Preparing doesn't automatically take you there, of course, but you must do it anyway. Otherwise, like the lottery winners who lost it all because they weren't prepared for their fortunes, you won't reach your true potential.

How many people have gotten married without being ready? Their marriages were miserable because they weren't prepared! Maybe they didn't get to know the person well enough first. (If you know the person really well—trust me—it's better!) Our divorce rate is so high because couples prepare for a beautiful wedding ceremony—but not for the marriage.

Now that you have a balanced life, you are prepared for the next level. You are prepared for the best life—a life of promise fulfilled. You are ready, my friend.

Here's to your balanced life!

Look for these logos and brands daily when shopping for financial and educational services:

ABI-Anis Blemur Institute:
Now A Real Estate School, offering online and live courses and continuing education
Soon to become a fully Accredited Business School
Visit us at www.abinstitute.org

AB Consulting & Accounting Services:
Business Planning, Incorporation, and Accounting
Visit us at www.abfinancials.com

ABFinancials.com:
Financial Planning, Life, Health, and Variable annuities

AB Tax Center:
Tax services for individuals, businesses and estate planning www.abfinancials.com/taxpreparation

AB Realty:
SuperTree Realty
Real Estate Going Global, invite all to invest and rest wealthy!
www.abfinancials.com/realestate

Join our Club! a great network to learn, have fun,
and . . . make lots of money:
The AB Club
www.theabclub.com
We never cease to search for motivated agents
and inspired leaders to join our teams, worldwide.
Thanks!

Anis Blemur "La Gestion des Affaires"

ABL—A Balanced Life Workbook

Educational Worksheet

Current Education Status & Future Goals

For each item on the list, put an "x" in the section that applies to you.

If the item has a blank line, fill out which area of study you would like to pursue in that category.

These will be your goals for the education portion of your balanced life.

	now	next year	2 years	5 years	10 years	20 years
None GED High School Diploma Associates Degree: _____ Bachelors Degree: _____ Masters Degree: _____ Doctorate Degree: _____ Licenses: _____ Certificates: _____ Other: _____						

Questionnaire for Currently Enrolled Students

If you are currently enrolled in schooling, after completing high school, please answer the following questions.

1. What is your major?

    _____

    _____

    _____

2. Is your major something you love to do? Or did you choose it for different reasons? Explain.

    _____

    _____

    _____

3. Have you ever changed your major? If yes, what was your major previously & why did you change it?

    _____

    _____

    _____

4. How far along are you & towards what degree, license, or certificate?

_____

_____

_____

_____

5. Do you already know what your career is going to be? If yes, what is it?

_____

_____

_____

6. Do you already have a job set up for when you finish your schooling?

_____

_____

_____

Questionnaire for Previously Enrolled Students

If you were previously enrolled in schooling after high school but aren't at the moment, please answer the following questions.

1. How long ago were you enrolled in schooling? What was your major & was it a degree, license, or certificate?

_____

_____

_____

2. Did you complete the schooling? If no, why did you stop, how far along were you & do you plan on going back to complete it?

_____

_____

_____

3. If you completed your schooling, have you started your career? If yes, what do you do for a living? If no, do you plan on going back to study something else?

_____

_____

_____

4. If you were previously enrolled in schooling, but you never finished & you have no intentions of going back, what are you currently doing as a career? Are you financially stable?

_____

_____

_____

5. If you are not financially stable, what do you plan on doing if not going back to school to further your knowledge or learn a trade?

_____

_____

_____

Questionnaire for Individuals Who Have Never Been Enrolled

If you have never been enrolled in any type of schooling after high school, please answer the following questions.

1. Why have you never been enrolled in schooling after high school?

    _____

    _____

    _____

2. If you have never been enrolled in courses due to financial issues, did you know that financial aid is available to you?

    _____

    _____

    _____

3. Do you have intentions of pursuing an education to further your knowledge or learn a trade? If not, do you have a plan for your future? Explain.

    _____

    _____

    _____

4. If you are not interested in schooling because you already have a career, are you financially stable within your career? Or are you just barely getting by but have no time to pursue your education?

_____

_____

_____

TIP: It is never too late to enhance your education. It doesn't matter if you are middle-age and you've never been enrolled in schooling. Education is probably the most powerful weapon, which can be used to change the world. Why not begin with your life?

ABL—A balanced Life Workbook

Emotional Worksheet

Relationships

The relationships you have with the people closest to you have a great effect on your emotions. In the graph below, mark an "x" in the box that best suits your current relationship with the person listed.

	N/A	Irreparable	Needs Improvement	Fair	Good	Excellent
Mother						
Father						
Sister(s)						
Brother(s)						
Spouse						
Children						
Best Friend(s)						
Co-worker(s)						
Boss						
Other: _____						
Other: _____						

Relationship Questionnaire

Answer the following questions about your relationships.

1. If you answered "Irreparable" or "Needs Improvement" for any relationship, do you understand that this can cause great strain on your emotions?

    _____

    _____

    _____

2. Why do you believe that your relationship is "Irreparable?" Forgiveness is one of the keys to stable emotions.

    _____

    _____

    _____

3. Are you working on those relationships that "Need Improvement?" If not, you should definitely start as soon as possible.

    _____

    _____

    _____

4. If you answered "Fair" or "Good" to any relationship, what can you do to make it an "Excellent" relationship and why haven't you taken action already?

_____

_____

_____

TIP: Try to get all of your immediate relationships as close to "Excellent" as possible. If you are in good standing with all the people you are closest with and come into contact with everyday, your life will be much more stress free.

Debt

Financial debt can also have a lot to do with our emotional well being. If we're in debt, that can definitely take a toll on how we feel about life. In the graph below, mark an "x" in the box that best describes how long it will take you to be debt free, if applicable.

	N/A	1 Year or Less	2-3 Years	4-5 Years	6-9 Years	10 Years or More
Credit Card Debt Hospital Bills Car Note Student Loans Mortgage Other: _____ Other: _____						

Debt Questionnaire

Answer the following questions about your debts.

1. If you mostly answered, "1 Year or Less," you are on the right track. Do you have a budget you set to achieve these goals? Explain.

   _____

   _____

   _____

2. If you mostly answered, "2-3 Years" or "3-5 Years," have you met with a financial advisor to try consolidating loans or paying off a larger part of the balance so you can pay off your debts faster?

   _____

   _____

   _____

3. If you mostly answered, "5-9 Years," have you considered hiring a personal accountant to keep you on track with your goals?

   _____

   _____

   _____

4. If you answered "10 Years or More," do you have a life insurance policy? If not, you should consider it. In case of death, you wouldn't want to burden anyone in your family with your debt.

_____

_____

_____

> **TIP:** Regardless how long it will take you to pay your debt, brace yourself, pace yourself, & don't let it overwhelm you. Have a plan and don't stop saving money for a rainy day. DON'T let the debt consume you, life goes on!

Health

Health is a very big component when it comes to our emotional well being. Mark an "x" in the box that represents how often you do what is listed.

	N/A	Never	Rarely	50/50	Often	Always
Work Out Eat Healthy Get Check-Ups Other: _____ Other: _____						

Health Questionnaire

Please answer the following questions about your health.

5. If you answered mostly answered "Never," are you often tired or cranky during the day? Do you feel drained most of the time? Unhealthy exercise & eating habits can make it much harder to get through the day without getting stressed or overwhelmed. Make it your mission to improve your habits.

_____

_____

_____

6. If you answered mostly "Rarely" or "50/50," you are on the right track. Can you dedicate yourself to changing that answer to "Often" or "Always"?

_____

_____

_____

7. If you answered mostly "Often" or "Always," you are right where you need to be. Does working out & eating right give you energy to make it through the day?

_____

_____

_____

> **TIP: Eating right & working out is beneficial in so many ways. It not only helps regulate weight, it helps normalize blood sugar, lowers chances for disease, helps you sleep better at night, energizes you through the day, helps balance your mood and emotions. Try to form healthy eating and exercise habits**

Spirituality Worksheet

Spirituality

Spirituality plays a big role in achieving a balanced life.

1. Mark an "x" in the box that best suits your beliefs.

   ☐ Atheist
   ☐ Deist
   ☐ Judaist
   ☐ Christian
   ☐ Buddhist
   ☐ Other: _____

2. Based on your beliefs, do you follow the:
   (Mark [Y] for yes or [N] for no.)

   __ Rules
   __ Rituals
   __ Honoring
   __ Prayer/ Worship Time
   __ "Book" Reading—If yes, which worship book?

   _____

   __ Sacrifices

3. Regardless of your belief, do you believe in life after death? Explain.

_____

_____

_____

4. If yes, how do you see or prefer after-life?

   ☐ Reincarnated—Back on Earth
   ☐ Wandering Around
   ☐ In Heaven, as described in the "Bible"

5. Do you expect a glorious body or the same "you" in your after-life? Explain.

_____

_____

_____

6. If yes, what preparation do you now do to receive your glorious body, later?

_____

_____

_____

7. Do you consider yourself a religious person? Explain why or why not.

_____

_____

_____

8. How often do you go to your place of worship? Mark an "x" in the box that best describes your answer.

    ☐ Once a Month or Less
    ☐ Twice a Month
    ☐ Three times a Month
    ☐ Four times a Month or More

9. Do you observe the basic rules or your place of worship? Mark an "x" in the box that represents how often you do what is listed.

	N/A	Never	Rarely	50/50	Often	Always
Tithing Giving Bible/Other Sacred Book(s) _____ Study Activities						

10. What are the commandments of your religion/ beliefs? (For example, for Christians: the "Ten Commandments")

_____

_____

_____

11. Do you pray? Mark an "x" in the box that represents how often you do what is listed.

	N/A	Never	Rarely	50/50	Often	Always
Pray						

12. "Prayer Changes Things!" Is this sentence:

☐ True
☐ False
☐ I Don't Know

13. Do you believe in miracles?

☐ Yes
☐ No
☐ I Don't Know

Based on your answers, please answer the following questions:

	N/A	Not At All	Sort Of	50/50	Yes	Definitely
Am I a religious person? Did this exercise help me to determine where I stand with my Spiritual Life? Am I less confused about this topic than before? Do I need more help with my spiritual beliefs/ knowledge? I want to know who GOD is:						

ABL—A Balanced Life Workbook

Financial Worksheet

The financial worksheet may be the most important one for most of you. As I was putting it together I realized it encompassed all areas of life. However, there are choices to be made here! Now think of me as your Coach, your financial coach, going over all your choices with you, when you, only you, have to set some priorities

For each item on the list, put 1 next to the most important one, 2 to the next more important and so on. Cross out the one that are not important.

	Now	Next Year	2 Years	5 Years	10 Years	20 Years
Buy a car						
Lease a car						
Buy a new car						
Buy a house						
Buy a second/vacation house						
Move to retirement community						
Buy expensive clothes						
Trade up to better house						
Renovate your house						
Redecorate; buy new furniture/ appliances						
Pay your college loans						
Get further education/ training						
Send your kids to private school						
Send your kids to college						
Look for new job within the same industry						
Relocate to a new area						
Make a career transition						
Start a business/Invest in a business						

	Now	Next Year	2 Years	5 Years	10 Years	20 Years
Buy/improve health insurance						
Buy/improve life insurance						
Create/add to savings account						
Invest in stocks						
Invest in bonds						
Invest in bonds						
Invest in mutual funds						
Invest in real estate (other than your home)						
Invest in art/collectibles						
Invest in gold						
Take a vacation						
Entertain						
Send your kids to camp						
Make pension plan contributions						
Create a trust						
Donate gifts to charity						
Help aging parents/in-laws						
Give gifts to other relatives						
Pay for health care (self or family)						
Pay for long-term care						

While going to this tedious exercise (Fun!) I want you to make the difference between consumption expenses and productive expenses. Note their values and importance all along

You need funds for your main objectives, don't you?

Based on your estimate, write down below the amount you will need, this year or in the future, if necesary

Funds Needed

Objective	Now	Next Year	2 Years	5 years	10 years	20 years
___	___	___	___	___	___	___
___	___	___	___	___	___	___
___	___	___	___	___	___	___
___	___	___	___	___	___	___
___	___	___	___	___	___	___
___	___	___	___	___	___	___
___	___	___	___	___	___	___
___	___	___	___	___	___	___

Surely, you don't have all the cash needed

Estimate the amount of money you think will be available from your salary and your spouse's salary, investment income, selling stocks and so forth, in each of these years: Be realistic! That's what I mean

Available Funds

Objective	Now	Next Year	2 Years	5 years	10 years	20 years
___	___	___	___	___	___	___
___	___	___	___	___	___	___
___	___	___	___	___	___	___
___	___	___	___	___	___	___
___	___	___	___	___	___	___
___	___	___	___	___	___	___
___	___	___	___	___	___	___
___	___	___	___	___	___	___

Apparently you are going to need more funds, don't you? Well! Can you think of some places where you going to find them? *Now, let's rule out one possible source: Bank robbery!*

(Possibilities: career changes; working longer hours; getting additional part-time work; reducing lifestyle spending; liquidating some investments; shifting from growth- to income-oriented investments; getting a home-equity loan or reverse mortgage; getting help from family members; borrowing against your pension plan. Of course, strategies that involve borrowing just defer the problem; they don't solve it.)

List your choices here:

_____

_____

_____

_____

Do you have (own) anything at all? Maybe, maybe not! But wait! Just list them all if you do. They are your valuables, your Assets

Major Assets

Description	Location	Date Acquired	Value Then	Value Now

Now or later you will have to deal with some major financial challenges

I cannot list them all here; however, you should think of them while working on you financial planning and budgeting. For example, buying or leasing a car; or it's maintenance!

Let's do this exercise. Ready? I,_____, need $_____ to replace my "bobo" car (oops! Sorry!) And I need $_____ to maintain it. In addition, the costs to run this car Will be, on a yearly basis, $_____. This amount includes, but not limited to, Fuel $_____, auto insurance $_____ I have $_____ as down payment to complete the purchase.

Additional Purchases

Plan to Renovate the house: The total costs will be $_____; I will get the money from savings and borrow the balance at a cost of $_____ a month.

Buy furniture, The total costs will be $_____; I will get the money from savings and borrow the balance at a cost of $_____ a month.

Buy appliances: The total costs will be $_____; I will get the money from savings and borrow the balance at a cost of $_____ a month.

Buy electronic items (home computer, video camera, music system), The total costs will be $_____; I will get the money from savings and borrow the balance at a cost $_____ a month.

Credit Costs

For all your loans and credit cards, list the outstanding balance and interest rate.

	Balance	Interest Rate	Interest
Amount			
Car Loan	_____	_____	_____
Home Mortgage	_____	_____	_____
Second Mortgage	_____	_____	_____
Home-Equity Loan	_____	_____	_____
Student Loans	_____	_____	_____
Credit Card #1	_____	_____	_____
Credit Card #2	_____	_____	_____
Credit Card #3	_____	_____	_____
Debit or Smart Card	_____	_____	_____
Other	_____	_____	_____

How much interest do you pay in an average month? $_____

How does the interest rate compare to the return you get on your savings and investments? ☐ Higher ☐ Lower

Could you save money by consolidating loans or paying off a larger part of the balance? ☐ Yes ☐ No

Home Costs

This year, you estimate that your monthly rent or mortgage payment (including insurance and real estate taxes) will be $_____ a month, $_____ for the year; your utility bills will be about $_____, fuel costs about $_____. If you're buying a house for the first time, or adding a second home, you estimate that you'll need $_____ for a down payment, plus mortgage fees and closing costs of $_____, and the change will reduce/ increase your monthly housing costs by $_____.

Second/ Vacation Home

This year you plan to buy/ rent a second or vacation home: Rent a house/ apartment/ time share unit for ____ weeks at $_____ a week.

Buy a house/ apartment/ condominium unit/ time share unit for a total of $_____, of which this year you'll have to pay $_____ (down payment) and ____ monthly payments of $_____ each, plus one-time closing costs of $_____. This second/ vacation home needs $_____ of furnishing, decoration, and renovation, of which you plan to spend $_____ this year.

Investments

How would you describe your level of investment knowledge?

_____

What would you say is your investment style?

_____

How would you rate your past performance in saving and investing?

_____

Your investments were described earlier in the "assets" listing. Do you have a "savings cushion" or at least six months' income?

Yes

No, but will accumulate it by the end of the year

No, but will accumulate it by the end of next year

Once you have the savings in place, you plan to invest about $_____ this year, $_____ next year, and $_____ the year after that, using this basic strategy:

_____

_____

_____

_____

For your existing investments, did they meet your goals and expectations (revising the goals and expectations if they are not realistic)? ☐ Yes ☐ No

Steps you plan to take to improve your investments results:

_____

_____

_____

Family Financial Challenges

This year you expect to have family related costs in these areas:

- Maternity/ Childbirth
- Childcare
- Education
- Other child-related expenses (camp, vacations)
- Gifts, loans, and sales within the family

Birth and Child Care

This year, you estimate that you will have $_____ in birth/ adoption expenses, of which $_____ will be reimbursed (for example, by your employer), and for which you can take a tax deduction or credit of $_____. You estimate that paid child care inside and outside your home will cost a total of $_____. You can estimate that you and/or your spouse will lose income of $_____ this year because of quitting a job or taking a leave of absence or unpaid leave.

Education Costs

This year, you estimate that you will spend $_____ on elementary/ secondary school tuition, $_____ for summer camp, $_____ for tutoring and lessons, and $_____ on college tuition for your kids. If you don't have any kids in college yet, you estimate that it will be ____ years before the first child enters college, and then there'll be a ____ year period when you have at least one child in college or graduate school. You plan to invest $_____ a year toward future education costs, and your basic investment strategy is:

_____

_____

_____

_____

Divorce (if applicable)

List the assets that you will transfer to your spouse as part of the financial arrangements for the divorce:

_____

_____

List the assets you will receive:

_____

_____

What arrangements will be made about the family home?

_____

_____

What arrangements will be made about pension rights?

_____

_____

What arrangements will be made about medical insurance?

_____

_____

You expect to pay/receive $_____ per month for spousal support (until _____), and to pay/receive $_____ per month (until _____) for child support.

What will you do if payments are not made promptly or in full?

_____

_____

Insurance

Do you consider your insurance coverage adequate?

Yes ☐ No, need more/ different coverage:

Action Agenda:

Buy $_____ of ___ year term insurance from (company):

_____ (agent or broker):

_____

Buy $_____ of whole life insurance from (company):

_____

(agent or broker):

_____

Add more homeowner's insurance: $_____ from

_____

Add more liability/ property coverage on auto policy: $_____ from: _____

_____

Anis Blémur

Buy disability insurance to replace ___% of your income, from:

_____

Buy health insurance, described as follows:_____
from:

_____

Buy Medigap Insurance Plan _____ from: _____

_____

Buy long-term care insurance, covering ___ years of care, with a benefit of $_____ institutional, $_____ home care, after a waiting period of ___, from:

_____

Taxes

What action steps have you completed?

Use your computer financial planning program to gather tax information.

Review your checkbook, receipts, and other financial records; make a list of deductions and credits

Collect the forms and publications you need

Make an appointment with an accountant/ tax lawyer/ tax preparation service

File tax returns (or request for extension if necessary)

Which planning steps are right for you?

Shift income to other family members

Defer income (with pension plans, 401(k), etc.)

Buy/improve a home

Make charitable gifts

Give gifts to family members and friends

Set up life insurance trust

Set up other kinds of trusts

Invest in tax-free investments

Put more investment emphasis on growth, less on income

☐ Other (describe):

Health Care Planning

This year, you have adequate health insurance coverage under an employer plan, have to pay \$_____ a year on health insurance coverage for yourself and your family. You already have disability insurance, which costs \$_____ a year, want to add disability insurance, and can pay up to \$_____ a year, don't have and don't want disability insurance. You already have Medigap insurance, which costs \$_____ a year, want to add Medigap insurance and can pay up to \$_____ a year, don't have and don't want Medigap insurance. You already have long-term care insurance, which costs \$_____ a year, want to add long-term care insurance, and can pay up to \$_____ a year, don't have and don't want long-term care insurance.

For each of these documents, indicate if you have them (and if so, where they are); if you don't have them, indicate if you want to add them.

	Have	Location	Want to Add	Don't Want
Living Will				
Health Care Proxy				
Advanced Designation of Guardian				
Retirement Planning				

If your parents or in-laws are still alive, list the ways (financial and personal) you are involved in their health care and financial planning: _____.

Indicate the action steps you intend to take for your own elder planning:

	Don't Want	Want	Action	Date of Action
Incapacity Planning				
Signing up for Medicare				
Buying Medigap Insurance				
Medicaid Planning				
Buying long-term care insurance				
Fixing up home				
Moving into special house				
Getting home health care				

Estate Planning

Explain your basic estate-planning strategy and your basic intentions for how your property should be disposed of:

Indicate the status of these legal documents:

	Have	Location	Don't Want	Want	Action
Will					
Trust					
DPA					
Living Will					
Health Care					
Proxy					
Advance					
Designation of Guardian					

I want _____ to be my executor and _____ to be my durable power of attorney agent (if applicable). He/she/they is/are aware that they have been named; is/are willing and able to serve; and knows/know about my financial status and my wishes.

Coping with Problems

Over and above the normal wear and tear of financial life, some people encounter additional challenges that require an extra ration of information and planning techniques.

Career Transition (if applicable)

(Involuntary transition) You expect to get a severance package worth $_____, including $_____ in cash, $_____ in benefits, and $_____ worth of outplacement assistance, plus $_____ in unemployment insurance benefits.

You expect that finding a new job will take ____ weeks.

You project that the job search will cost $_____ (counseling, resumes, new wardrobe, travel, phone calls, and so forth).

In addition to savings, you plan to use these sources of income: unemployment insurance, loans from friends, family, temporary work in your field, temporary work outside your field.

Disability (if applicable)

Based on your own feelings and professional advice, you think that this period of disability will last: under 3 months, 3-6 months, 6 months-1 year, over 1 year, and you think it: will, will not reoccur.

(Going back to your old job): ☐
You think you can go back to work after you recover
You think you can go back to work if accommodations are made (schedule, transportation, adaptive equipment)
You don't think you can go back to the old job, but can do other work for the same employer
You think you'll need a different kind of job

Overall Action Agenda

Which professional advisors do you need to hire?
Lawyer ☐ Accountant ☐ Financial Planner ☐ Broker ☐ Insurance Agent ☐ Real Estate Agent ☐ Geriatric Care Manager ☐ Other: _____

Which steps are you going to take this month?

Save Money: $_____

Invest: $_____ in _____

Make major purchase: _____

Get legal/ accounting/ financial planning/ investment/ insurance or other professional advice from _____ about _____

Pay annual/ estimated/ real estate taxes of approximately $_____ or get a tax refund of approximately $_____, which will be used for _____

Career change: _____

Which steps are you going to take in the next three months?

Save Money: $_____

Invest: $_____in _____

Make major purchase: _____

Get legal/ accounting/ financial planning/ investment/ insurance or other professional advice from _____ about _____

Pay annual/ estimated/ real estate taxes of approximately $_____ or get a tax refund of approximately $_____, which will be used for _____

Career change: _____

Which steps are you going to take in the next year?

Save Money: $_____

Invest: $_____ in _____

Make major purchase: _____

Get legal/ accounting/ financial planning/ investment/ insurance or other professional advice from _____ about _____

Pay annual/ estimated/ real estate taxes of approximately $_____ or get a tax refund of approximately $_____, which will be used for _____

Career change: _____

Which steps are you going to take in the next five years?

Save Money: $_____

Invest: $_____ in _____

Make major purchase: _____

Get legal/ accounting/ financial planning/ investment/ insurance or other professional advice from _____ about _____

Pay annual/ estimated/ real estate taxes of approximately $_____ or get a tax refund of approximately $_____, which will be used for _____

Career change: _____

I am here for you! My office is here for you! My staff is here for you!

You may need to hire a few professionals, now or later. Do not take the risk of not having a financial road map. Start working on it now. Hire one or more professional advisors, Lawyer, Accountant, Financial Planner, and/or Insurance Agent; take a few steps ahead today: Start saving! Invest today, start paying taxes in advance; make a phone call today and inquire about College funds for tomorrow. Keep walking . . . Don't stop . . .

You Are On Your Way to A Balanced Life!